# Pour a Libation

Also by Dawn Colsey and published by Ginninderra Press

*Jacaranda Song* (Pocket Poets)

Dawn Colsey

# Pour a Libation

# Acknowledgements

Some of these poems have appeared, not necessarily in identical form, in the following publications: *Friendly Street Annual Reader* in most years from 1989; *Writers on Parade*, Journal of Kensington and Norwood Writers' Group, 1-7; Haiku Bindii Japanese forms journal Journeys; *Willowlight* 2015; *World's Best Tanka* 2012; *Guardian* (Anglican Diocese of Adelaide); *Seasons of a New Heart*, Effective Living Centre; *Fruit of Sophia* and other Sophia journals; *Windfall* 2015.

Awards: Kaji Aso Competition Boston – Haibun; Friendly Street Poem of the Month, July 2011, for 'Deepwater Blobfish'; 'World's Best Tanka 2012 for tsunami; 'For Alison' included in The Rev'd Lesley McLean's PhD on Alison Gent; 'Replace Caged Birds with Flowers' Friendly Street Poem of the Month, April 2014.

My thanks to Ginninderra Press for their generous service to poetry publication in Adelaide and beyond.

I am grateful to Elaine Barker, my Friendly Street mentor in 2012, for her encouragement and rigour; to Jenny Wightman of Sophia Women Writing about Themselves, who edited some of the poems, and to the women of that diverse group; to my creative writing friends in several groups including A Passion of Poets, Sophia Women's Poetry Circle and Kensington and Norwood Writers' Group.

*Pour a Libation*
ISBN 978 1 74027 916 1
Copyright © text Dawn Colsey 2015
Front cover photograph: The Metropolitan Museum of Art, New York, The Collection Online, through Art Resource, INA 0601797 ART 426148 *Antigone Pouring a Libation over the corpse of her brother Polynices*, William Henry Rinehart (American, Union Bridge, Maryland 1825–1874 Rome) Marble. Photograph by Jerry L. Thompson
Back cover photograph: Baptism of Alfred Manifold, March 2014, St Edward's Church, Kensington Gardens, with thanks to the Manifold family

First published 2015 by
**GINNINDERRA PRESS**
PO Box 3461 Port Adelaide 5015 Australia
www.ginninderrapress.com.au

# Contents

| | |
|---|---|
| **the beloved place** | **9** |
| Welcome to country | 11 |
| A Derwent Lakeland coloured pencil landscape | 12 |
| I drink Sevenhill wine | 13 |
| The vine pruner | 14 |
| Wardrobe bells | 15 |
| Garden of the old farmhouse at Easter | 16 |
| The raw art of landscape | 17 |
| The well | 18 |
| Himeji Garden sequence | 19 |
| haiku, brief glimpses | 23 |
| I enter the tree cathedral | 25 |
| a way to die | 26 |
| Lakeside dreaming | 27 |
| **Ah! If I have a heart…** | **29** |
| Three poems on Patricia Piccinini's work *Once upon a time…* | 31 |
| Replace caged birds with flowers | 34 |
| The outsider | 35 |
| Fragile life | 36 |
| How to sing like a magpie | 37 |
| When the children leave | 38 |
| Hierarchy at the bird bath | 39 |
| Bitumen-grey duck | 40 |
| Peak hour, rainy Saturday | 41 |
| Mist, Sevenhill morning | 42 |
| Haibun, Goolwa | 44 |
| Wild and windy beach holiday | 45 |
| Wishing him wholeness | 46 |
| Life goes on | 47 |
| Wounded partisan priest | 48 |

**What makes a difference to destiny?**     **49**

| | |
|---|---|
| News of new life (at not quite 8 weeks!) | 51 |
| Dancing with Eleanor aged 12½ weeks | 52 |
| A little girl | 54 |
| Walking Grace to school at 5½ years old | 55 |
| Grace's rainbow | 56 |
| No restful Saturday morning | 57 |
| An earthworm on the back of my hand | 58 |
| Two sneeze poems | 59 |
| Innocent cake | 60 |
| One more year | 61 |
| Field hospital, conflict zone | 62 |
| Miriam of Nazareth speaks today | 63 |
| Breaking down barriers | 64 |
| The Big Issue | 65 |
| 'Short Back and Sides' | 66 |
| Poppy | 67 |
| Seeing good things in the blackout | 69 |
| Thoughts on an autumn Saturday | 70 |
| Valentine's date 14.2.14 | 71 |
| A blue globe of sky | 72 |
| Stop getting at me | 73 |
| Final exam | 74 |

**What will express love, shared?**     **75**

| | |
|---|---|
| Jacaranda, symbol of seasons | 77 |
| For Alison | 78 |
| Let us look with Christmas eyes | 79 |
| Thoughts while selling badges for the Christmas Bowl 2013 | 80 |
| At one moment in time and always: the Christmas Eucharist | 82 |
| Christmas morning | 83 |

| | |
|---|---|
| Sevenhill at Easter | 84 |
| a tanka for the Triduum* | 85 |
| The reality of God's presence to me | 86 |
| In the Sophia dry-land garden after a week of fires | 88 |
| Day of the Magdalen | 89 |
| Wedding music | 91 |
| Tanka: six months after the flood | 92 |
| Teacher | 93 |
| To drown or not to drown | 94 |
| haiku, tanka, brief glimpses | 95 |
| Light upon silk | 96 |
| haiku, tanka, brief glimpses | 97 |
| Woman priest to woman dying | 98 |
| The invitation of the spiral | 99 |

## Poem of Dedication

my libation, words,
their source mystery,
an outpouring
for the Holy One,
mediated through human mind.

# the beloved place

# Welcome to country

At the National Poetry Festival, Goolwa

Auntie Eileen, Ngarrindjerri woman,
tells us, the poets,
'The Christian missionaries would not allow us
to use language.
So for two years now
I have been relearning language.
There is no poetry in language,
so I will just speak.
I welcome you to our traditional lands.'

Choosing carefully she pours out the words,
revering the river, the sand dunes, the ocean.
No poetry? No? Where did it flee
with language forbidden?
To river, to ocean?
She looks out where Hindmarsh Island bridge
links land to island in a descending curve.
All her language seems like poetry,
a language of redemption.

# A Derwent Lakeland coloured pencil landscape

I had only twelve of the precious colours,
envied my cousin Rosalie, who had twenty-four,
or was it forty-eight? Yesterday
the anniversary of her early death,
and I ever regretful
I did not make the journey she requested
to visit her before she died.

This journey's mine, through soft winter sky,
the pale blue lit by sun/cloud brightness.
White was one of the twelve,
grey for their underbellies.
Soft brown, a touch of black's deep shadow,
and emerald green,
for winter grasses pushing through.

I seek my favourite green, bluish and whitish.
Did it have its own name?
Most worn because most treasured.
Yellow for a burst of flowers in a hedge.
Pink? Keep that for morning sky,
and purple would be unseasonal.
Red and orange, now that I've arrived,
for a vivid sunset, closing
a radiant afternoon.

# I drink Sevenhill wine

soft merlot, velvet red.
It takes me to the beloved place –
prayer within the walls,
the work of vines outside –
wine-making in slow time –
patience, stability infused into fruit –
bliss made liquid
to ease the heart.

# The vine pruner

His coat on a post,
now that the day is warmer,
he makes his painstaking way
along the rows.
He sizes up each vine,
decides exactly where
to place each cut.

While branches and last leaves
drop to earth,
roots already rest
until sap surges in spring,
and stem feeds shoot and fruit,
nature's work-
equally meticulous.

# Wardrobe bells

The loft rooms of the old Jesuit college
have all been spruced up,
redesigned, repainted,
altogether refurbished.

When the wire coat-hangers
among the new plastic ones
tinkle in the wardrobe,
I hear the old wardrobe's ghost
with its many wire hangers
ringing like bells
recalling past times.

# Garden of the old farmhouse at Easter

It could be Joseph of Arimathea's garden.
In early dappled light
birch trees scatter earth
with their treasure of gold coins,
not the silver of betrayal.

The path could lead to a tomb,
old stones fixed in place
many decades ago, and iron
strong in spite of age,
for plough, gate and bolt.

The year may be dying into autumn,
but here is living water,
bread of life,
freshness, new hope
where I encounter You.

# The raw art of landscape

From Auburn I drive south
towards a rounded hill
yellow with canola.
It fills the foreground,
cuts a hard edge
against cloudless blue.
A single road sign imposes.

When I stand outside the car
I am the dwarfed figure
alone
in a Jeffrey Smart painting.

# The well

Himeji Garden, Adelaide

Where water trickles constantly
over the edge of the sandstone block,
symbolic of a well,
bees alight gently,
take tentative sips
at the water's edge.

If old or weary
they risk drowning.
I grieve their sad corpses,
wrapped in white algae shrouds
round the base
of the well stone.

Praise to you, God of bees
and wells, water
and purple bells of jacaranda.
Praise that in such detail
I can perceive You.

# Himeji Garden sequence

my camera forgotten
I take pictures
with eyes and words

sunny autumn afternoon
low curving pine branches
create caves of shade

graceful arc of a reed
holds a round-woven web
a dragonfly
darts by
uncaught

the lake, *s'ensui*,*
sends reflected ripples
up to the glistening pine

a duck keeps half an eye
on the poet
in case she changes
pen
for bread crusts

pine opens great cones above
the watering lake
will seeds grow?


\* a lake in the form of *shin*, 'heart' or 'soul'

so much clipping to control
one pine reaches high
and free

a child runs past
long lily leaves
wave in her breeze

people arrive
crowding the garden
children want fish, tadpoles, turtles
a parrot dips low
dive-bombing all back to silence

dipping fingers in the lake
'they're biting me'
calls the Maori boy
red carp not so lethargic
in their gliding

two ducks circle
alternate their head-bobbing
a water dance

children have fed the ducks
and fled to something new
shade and silence
remain for me

the deer scarer bumps
tap clunk
in my mind
deer feet
clatter away

Easter lilies are past their best
though Lent
is still the season

foreign bella donna
lovely woman
though not geisha

nerines in delicate flower
no lush roses
to outdo them

no drowned bees
at the well this year
they have taught their children
to sip at the edge

bees hover
over water lily leaves
to drink with dry feet

maple leaves dry out
winged pods prepare
to shed seeds

among dry reeds
blue flicker
dragonfly, not flame

straight in line
with lofty palm's drooping fronds
the lantern
*misakidoro**
lifts its upcurved edges

* a water-viewing lantern

## haiku, brief glimpses

Kalgoorlie eucalypts
seeking water
bear leaves tinged with gold

one house burnt
one saved, protected only
by prayer flags

snowflakes drift
along the gutters
in my street
Manchurian pear blossoms
greet spring

in morning ritual
I switch on the lamp
paws pad across the doona
I stretch out my arm
a chin rests on my hand
from the throat love vibrates

we sing for the feast day
Michael and All Angels
high on the garden arch
Angel Face rose
blooms in perfection

wisteria bunches
sparkle with raindrops
spring's chandeliers

grey sky reflects
among red leaves
in the bird bath

bleached grass
on red earth
autumn thirsts for rain

are you grateful for night rain?
a scabious flower nods a mauve-petalled 'yes'
where it pushes singly from dampened soil

# I enter the tree cathedral

Victoria Avenue, Unley Park,
its name so establishment,
its leaves so tender with spring's dappled light.
Plane tree tendrils reach down to caress,
leftover seedpods play,
bobbing as I pass.

## a way to die

fall from the sky
and be received
by a foreign field
of sunflowers

## Lakeside dreaming

Clare Country Club is grand,
but a simple wooden jetty
takes me out above the edge of the lake,
a Sea of Galilee in the Clare Valley.
Tannin water reflects clouds,
ripples to the shore,
gum-leaf strewn.

I am glad to hear the frog's voice,
a bird's protest,
and a kookaburra's laugh,
in case this conference for clergy
is all too serious.

Could there be fish?
Not strong and bony St Peter's fish
for impulsive darting in;
gentle minnows perhaps,
nosing among leaves.
A plop. Something breaks the surface,
falling from a Zacchean tree,
or rising up to catch a word of beatitude.

# Ah! If I have a heart...

# Three poems on Patricia Piccinini's work *Once upon a time...*

Exhibition at the Art Gallery of South Australia, June 2011

## Deepwater blobfish

*psychrolutes marcidus*

I would not like my name
if I were capable of knowing.
I am all gelatinous body,
colourless, or you could say white-pink
as though drained of blood and life,
but alive, flopped like mucoid detritus
on the ocean's bed.

My squint eyes form a half smile
as my prey passes close
to my blubbery mouth.
I have no muscles.
My languorous lips open
for lobster or bottom-feeding fish
and I imbibe.

There must be more to life
than these black depths,
more than intake and excretion.
Ah, if I have a heart
I cannot speak of it breaking.
It melts constantly
with yearning.

## Eulogy

He embodies compassion. His cupped hands
cradle the helpless blobfish
removed from the sea's depth
to alien air: the tail dangles,
the mouth flops, though faintly smiling,
and the eye wonders at the touch of kindness.

The man kneels low on the ground,
his head bowed over the passive burden.
He offers its vulnerable pink-white flesh
to the eternal possibility that with death,
we, all creatures, do not
totally die.

## The long-awaited

Trust and tenderness rest together.
An ordinary boy sleeps against the aged body
of an extraordinary elderly creature.
A small hand comforts the head.
A short arm lies along an elongated arm/fin.
Both faces droop. Repose is deep,
longed for by the ancient one,
easily found by the young.

On short legs a boy's feet dangle in his shoes.
The well nourished old one stretches his ample belly
and lengthy fin to a many-toed tail/foot.
Half smiles suggest the osmosis of wisdom,
from grey-haired wrinkled brow,
into the future-dreaming man-child.

# Replace caged birds with flowers

I buy a frivolous Easter treat,
a birdcage painted lolly pink,
made of course in China,
with metal flowers and leaves
moulded between the bars.
It's meant to hold a pot plant.
I add a vase of autumn roses,
pink and white Seduction.

What seduces me, crafted too in metal:
three birds perched on the outside.
I could wish all people held with bars,
their search for a free land stifled,
could gaze from outside, far beyond the cage,
as freedom's roses bloom within.

# The outsider

Her wild and pleading eyes seek trust.
Her face is thin with hunger,
her lean body furtive in every movement,
unwanted, knowing more of escape,
or flight to safety,
than of warmth, or compassion,
or an invitation to a home.

An edge-dweller,
she waits for the darkness of night,
lights out, others curled in bed.
She embodies the marginalised,
the one who slinks and peers
to see what she can safely steal.

When I enter into
her anonymous life,
she helps me know
how it feels to be an outcast.
Cat without a home.

# Fragile life

Daddy-long-legs, dangling
behind the bathroom door,
so fine and frail,
but sentient to my breath, my touch,
unlike your young one,
dead, I think, drifting
below you,
failed parachute strands.

# How to sing like a magpie

Take a few steps, head-bobbing
like an Egyptian god. After all,
you are bird-king in your own realm.
Pause. Raise your head, lift your wings
a little. Open your throat
and hear what tumbles out
as glorious sound.
Then, amazed, think, 'I'll try that again.'
And do it, for joy.

# When the children leave

grassy school sports grounds have a new population.
Sacred ibis take over; industrious families,
heads bent to their task,
curved backs brightly white,
legs, bills sharply black,
scavenge their meal, clean up
and recycle children's leftovers.

# Hierarchy at the bird bath

There's a sputtering and fluttering,
a swooping and hovering,
a spattering and splashing.
A dozen honey-eaters
have found the water level perfect
for a Sunday morning dip.
A single blackbird has no courage
to confront them.
A smaller yellow-brown fellow
cannot bring himself to land.
Reigning for the moment,
they take their turns
in threes and fours
with a sense of fairness
and queue-making
known only in the bird world.

# Bitumen-grey duck

In six p.m. traffic a duck
the colour of bitumen
scurries across North East Road,
feet urgent,
head purposeful.
A car brakes gently.
I lose sight of the duck
against the grey road surface
in the lanes of cars.
I hope it reached the median strip safely,
with just one more road to cross.

# Peak hour, rainy Saturday

silly galahs
flop to the road
in stopped traffic
to drink from puddles
the lights change
in fear
my heart
takes flight

# Mist, Sevenhill morning

White mist hangs heavy,
blending with white-grey sky.
Only a glimmer of light
makes the distinction.

I'm so glad my room
is at treetop height.
Small, round birds
flit in peppertree tops
among bunched yellow florets.
Are they robins?
Is that a blush on breast?
If so, the bird has quite a harem
of non-blushing wives.

To the west, mist hangs low,
the vines so wet,
their branches stark, dark
in their lined pattern:
vine row, grass row,
vines, grass,
soft, regular patchwork
quilting the earth.

Eastern rosellas,
heavy on topmost peppertree twigs,
swing and sip morning moisture,
their calls a quiet mutuality.
You could say a dull day,
no sun, no warmth.
You could say a soft morning,
quiet colours blending sky,
earth, vine, tree,
the gentlest painting
oversung with rich but sombre birdsong.
I feel grateful.

Sulphur-crested cockatoos
slice through misty air,
white wings, harsh cry
knife through tenderness.
Suddenly mist lifts,
the scene still soft,
but earth is carved from heaven
by the birds' passage.

# Haibun, Goolwa

## A different path from Basho's Narrow Road

Longing for peace and calm after such a busy month, I must escape from telephone, email, meetings. Goolwa draws me: quiet country town, extensive ocean beach. At night distant lights will twinkle along the coast. Monday morning dawns, a bright day of holiday sunshine. I pack the car…

> journeying…
> I drive through jacaranda air
> seeking stillness

The hilltop house is empty, cold, pristine though beautiful. A burst of yellow gazanias welcomes me. In the rear garden – natives in flower – Geraldton wax offers purple, and eremophila a paler mauve. In a vase these flowers give life to the solid wood of the family table. With dusk I begin to relax into the serenity of a sunset-painted sky. Darkness gathers. At night the storm breaks…

> battering winds…
> the house turbulent
> my thoughts whirl

Can a dwelling less than five years old, even in a raging gale, be so clamorous? The gentleness of sleep is inhabited by clattering, banging, flapping. Footsteps on the stairs? The ghost of architect, builder, painter? For two nights, two days, wind and rain lash. At last the wildness ceases. Sun warms. Birds sing…

> alone…
> high above the wide bay
> my loneliness becomes solitude

# Wild and windy beach holiday

Magpie, steadfast bird,
rejoices in the rain,
laughs into the wind.

# Wishing him wholeness

Little stone dragon has a broken-off foot.
I am not surprised.
Unsure of his powers,
we constantly move him
from windowsill to doorstop.
He's always glancing backwards,
sheepishly, with hooded eyes,
past scaly skin and folded wings
to where his curly tail
ends in an upward arrow.
Poor dragon.
I have no plaster cast
or mythic remedy
for your brokenness.

# Life goes on

Penny the peahen of Osmond Terrace
has become a communal pet.
With her old lady owner dead
and the very house demolished,
the bird boldly struts the streets,
looked out for, worried over by all,
yet keeping herself well fed.

She fossicks for cat's food, dog's food,
people's prize garden plants,
pecks at the wet green grass,
comes within feet of the curious,
keeps a lookout for cars.

On her head she wears a tiara
of delicate feathers in place.
She paces the pavement poised,
like a princess seeking
her prince.

# Wounded partisan priest

With metal claw
of such finesse
he elevates the Host.
In the east window's
streaming light
the fragile disk
becomes translucent.

In the same light source
the partisan's hand
is a dark silhouette.
Black and white conjoin
as never they did
in the cause which cost him
both hands, an eye
and shattered ear-drums.

No letter bomb could be
so powerful to express belief
as bread blessed
by steel fingers, spirit restored,
to feed all blacks, all whites,
all people.

# What makes a difference to destiny?

# News of new life (at not quite 8 weeks!)

Two months ago my daughter came to me with shining eyes,
said nothing, but filled my heart with the hope of secret knowing.

Now, bubbling with joy, her husband serious with responsibility,
they've told me of coming new life.

I pick garden flowers of welcome and blessing
to take to their home.

I look in the mirror with eyes made young
glimpsing a far-reaching future,
see beyond time's imprint
of laughter and tears
a blossom caught in my hair.

# Dancing with Eleanor aged 12½ weeks

Alone for the first time, I hold her,
bless her forehead with a kiss,
could never wish her more well-being,
this child in my arms,
eyes alert to take in the world.

Softly I start the music.
Aled Jones and his boyhood self
sing in duet,
'O holy night,
 the stars are brightly shining,
it is the night
of the dear Saviour's birth.'

The child is transfixed
as high, clear notes entwine us.
Holding her close to my face
I begin to move,
gently sway
in a dance of worship, thanksgiving
for life, her life, the life of the Child.

I sing, murmur, sing,
sound rises and falls.
She is embraced with song,
movement, peace.

My daughter comes in
to take her back home.
'She loves it,' I say,
greeting with laughter
her smile at unlikely partners.

'Thank you, Gran, for the dancing,'
she says for her daughter.
Thank you, God, for these moments of bliss.

# A little girl

Misha, subconsciously named
for Michael and Sharon,
resembles both her parents,
and neither, being her own small person.
Delightful, charming, she gives spontaneous hugs,
so boisterous she can knock Gran over.

Bright, with amazing memory,
she knows and sings the words
of every Disney song, in tune,
recites film dialogues too,
yet stubbornly ignores
request, command and threat
to leave the screen
and come for dinner;
and if forced, refuses to eat anything but meat.

A usual four-year-old she's not.
Unable to relate to others' feelings,
she bears the awkward label
'Autism Spectrum Disorder' or, more briefly, 'Asperger's'.
We are always more and other than our parents.

## Walking Grace to school at 5½ years old

'Can I keep this feather? Isn't it beautiful?'
She holds the magpie's gift,
caresses the soft tufts near the quill.
'You can,' I tell her, wondering why she doubts,
her mother fanatical for keeping clean.

'Every angel has white feathery wings' –
her next pronouncement.
'I've never seen one,' I venture.
'Oh, they all do,' with total assurance.

She skips ahead, chanting her morning song,
'Run, run, as fast as you can.
Can't catch me, I'm the gingerbread man.'
Come on, Granny. Come on.'
I check her little shoulders.
No feathers.
But still, an angel.

## Grace's rainbow

Dear Grace,
child of imagination and lightness of heart,
you painted me a rainbow of true colours
to keep in my kitchen gallery
of grandchildren's art.

When a strong, bright rainbow
stretched across the afternoon sky
above the garden's red autumn roses
on your birthday party day with friends,
you exclaimed in joy,
'The rainbow is my best present.'

May you always know
such joy and hope.

# No restful Saturday morning

Michael takes Sophie to her basketball game.
Sharon takes Misha to ballet.
I drive Grace to karate, my first experience.
At ten, she is slight, pale after a week of illness,
swamped in immaculate white trousers and shirt,
proud of her belt, orange after white,
then yellow-tipped, and yellow. Next will be green.
Her little girl's voice is thin. I can hardly hear her
on our car journey. But now we've arrived.
'Make sure you bow in the doorway,' she says,
grandparents' teacher genes showing forth.
I follow her, imitate her ceremonial bow.
'Who shall I speak to? Who's in charge?'
I whisper, as the class limbers up,
mostly older than her.
'He's my *sensai*,' nodding at a young man,
all six feet of him, belted in black.
'Cool, I'll keep an eye on her,' he assures me.
I know he will. Everything here is disciplined.
For an hour and a half Grace will thrive.
Gran will relax in her car, reading.
A restful time, after all.

# An earthworm on the back of my hand

Misha traces its shape with her finger.
'My hand is seventy-three years old,' I say,
conscious of the grey, distended vein.
'And mine is five,' she responds,
in triumph, boasting at her present age.
'Tomorrow my hand will be nine,' adds Sophie,
brightly, knowing I have remembered her birthday.

# Two sneeze poems

Misha's father shows her
how to offer a bowl of crisps
instead of picking up each one
and giving it to a guest in turn.
She brings the crisps
and sneezes over the whole bowl.
Now no one wants crisps from the four-year-old.

Grace, aged ten, at her grandpa's piano,
plays 'Silent Night'
with two hands well controlled.
A sudden sneeze interrupts her recital.
Unperturbed she plays on
to finish at 'Sleep in heavenly peace.'

# Innocent cake

After the baptism of Benjy, five months,
we gather in the park
for big brother's birthday,
Peter, aged three.
His cake is topped
with mounds of icing,
earthy brown and sepia,
a miniature bulldozer at work on top.
'It's a road-mending cake,'
a friend calls, clapping hands.

Dad makes a speech,
Mum lights candles.
We all sing the song.
Peter has eyes for the toy alone,
holds it with care, tests all moving parts.

Children hand out big helpings of cake.
Many guests say, 'No thanks.'
Inside hides the bright yellow 'dirt'.
The colouring bottle fell from mum's hands?
Or, though with a laugh, we fear
uranium yellowcake.

# One more year

A few token candles glow
on the chocolate cake.
Family and friends
begin 'Happy Birthday to you'.
Joyce, at one hundred and one today,
violinist, pianist, singer
in the fullness of her life,
now seems eager to sing
her own birthday song.

After a year of pain and immobility,
yet so alert she misses nothing,
she knows she could manage a rendering
more tuneful than all of ours.

# Field hospital, conflict zone

As the flare of sunset
ends an exhausting day
the Syrian doctor weeps.
She has no real means
to treat burnt children.
'The nations have forgotten my people.
It's as though we do not count.'
The world grows black.
Her cigarette glows and dims,
a pinpoint consolation.

# Miriam of Nazareth speaks today

Women of Israel and Palestine, Semites all,
do you not think of our common call?
There comes a time, I've found, to say
I do not understand, but I'll obey.

Keep your sons safe
in church or mosque or shuul
and teach them history's rule:
love of this narrow land,
its promise not yet fulfilled,
at what high price for all.

Hold husbands close indoors,
beware the Nablus road.
Put fish and bread into their hands.
Remember what He said?
Forbid them stones to hurl,
fragments of ancient streets,
and bullets eye-for-an-eye
for burning tyres' reek.

Let flaring fire die
with hatred's nails and thorns.
By three days' bitter grief
my sword-pierced heart was torn.

It's you who must teach peace,
show each small step along the way.
I thought my son had died in vain.
What hope for yours
of a resurrection day?

# Breaking down barriers

at seventy-one
Mary walks with her stick
on Tasmanian snow
to take hand-knitted beanies
to asylum seekers in detention.
The note from her knitting group
reads, 'Dear men, we hope that these beanies
warm your heads and your hearts.'

# The Big Issue

He stands silent and still
outside Haigh's expensive chocolate shop,
holding a single copy of the paper.
'How much?' I ask.
'Five dollars, lady.'

He points to the cover.
'It's not all about U2,' he says,
thinking I'm too old to be a fan.
'Look, the earthquake.'
'In New Zealand?'
'No.' He finds the words with a finger.
'In Armenia,' he points,
a drop of moisture
falling on the page.

I hand over the coins.
'Thank you. You have a nice day,' he says.
I will, feeling glad
I've had the chance
to buy the paper.
'And you too,' I add,
hoping he makes many sales
from those with dollars to spend
on chocolate.

## 'Short Back and Sides'

The gardener is a good man,
Hard-working, well-spoken, honest.
Carefully he notes what I want pruned.
His price seems reasonable.
I tell him what I don't want cut:
the long trails of fuchsia
where the honey-eaters sip.
Other things I don't think to mention:
little daisies growing where they like.
Let them be free.

But when the gardener gets to work
he is unstoppable,
his pruning a ravishment
to which I have agreed.
It feels like onslaught, pillage, rape.
I know that spring and rain
will make each plant renewed.
But he forgets the fuchsia
must be left to trail for honey-eaters.
Garden clean-up meant
away with daisies, ferns
bending over the path,
and succulents re-rooting where they will.

Oh garden,
I loved you overgrown,
testament to my careless indulgence.
I'll water and feed you
back to abundance.

# Poppy

I am small and simple, *papaver rhoeas*.
My scarlet petals light the cornfields
with bright flames.
I am red as blood,
and once a year you wear me
to remember those
who gave their lives for you.
Field poppy, corn poppy, Shirley too.
Perhaps she was the sweetheart
he left behind.

A garden flower,
*papaver nudicaule* is my name.
I love the cold
and bloom in winter,
bursting my crinkled colours
through hairy buds, unpromising,
yet fill your flower beds
with orange, yellow, salmon, white.
Iceland poppy, I would herald spring
if I could grow in frozen wastes.

Beware! Not for nothing
am I called *somniferum*,
the sleep-bearer.
For you risk sleep, delusion, living death.
I am the opium poppy,
resplendent in my frills,
my grey serrated leaves,
a cash crop lusted after
in Afghanistan, so widely smoked,

and legalised for the drug morphine,
the strong, the subtle.
I am painkiller, addict-maker,
to let you drift
from agony to numbness,
peace, oblivion.
Poets in history, cancer victims here today,
you have all embraced me,
*papaver somniferum*.
Sleep now, die now.

# Seeing good things in the blackout

Silence. Soft daylight.
My one candle reflected
in glass door and window.
Alert to the day's gifts,
I hear the throb
of luscious rain,
and cannot take hot coffee
for granted, or at all.

# Thoughts on an autumn Saturday

I write my poems by hand
my printer has sent my laptop
to Coventry

fine mist pervades
over autumn colours
an image in soft focus

on the high curve
of the rose arch a dove
perches in her roundness

from the pile of felled limbs,
shredded, rain-wet,
a perfume rises,
recalling the essence
of tree

# Valentine's date 14.2.14

So youthful, the two bodies,
entwined, absorbed.
She, fourteen perhaps,
and he no older.
A day for lovers,
fourteen or forty,
two thousand or two only.
An auspicious day,
14.2.2014

# A blue globe of sky

I find a blue balloon
bobbing in my garden
at a loose end
on its metallic string.
It's a blue globe of sky
complete with stars
and swirling comet tails,
an escapee from some cosmic party.

Since one of my pittosporum bushes
is beginning to die
– they're temperamental,
just up and go, you know -
I hang the balloon on a low branch
for a bit of cheer
in its moribund misery.
It wafts there in the breeze
for a day or so.

Next it's lurking in the carport,
still round and bubbly
but bedraggling on the ground.
So, I think, I'll pop it in the rubbish bin
just as it is,
cheerfully white and blue,
to give the East Waste bin man
a nice surprise,
a blue globe of sky
to brighten his odoriferous day,
on his boring, one-man,
big truck Thursday round.

## Stop getting at me

Good night, smart phone. You have too much to say.
I go to settings, tap sound, tap silent,
change vibrate always to vibrate never,
plug you into the charger.
Good night, phone.
Ah, peace.

# Final exam

With hair stuffed roughly
into a black beanie
labelled 'TRIPPIN',
and sippin'
on an energy drink
in a bright green can,
Jack sits his university exam.
The subject: Deviance 101.

What will express love, shared?

# Jacaranda, symbol of seasons

Jacaranda as the foreteller of Advent and the seasons which follow

Jacaranda's glorious purple, the tree's full embellishment,
foretells a coming, an Advent more meaningful
than summer's clear blue, and bright beach days;
the coming of a child, divine one in human form,
vulnerable enough to be at human mercy,
helpless enough for human mothering.

Greeted as a new king, for him jacaranda spreads her carpet,
worn threadbare over centuries, and renewed,
feasted on by bees preparing their honey gift
more rich than any gold.
Like frankincense from thurible,
my prayers of gratitude rise up unbidden.

The tree too, with perfume kindlier than myrrh for burial,
in her own season bears her fruits. By them we know her,
bell-clappers for December's carillon, castanets for a dance
    of joy,
and with her fern-like foliage, an epiphany,
as the new year's promise begins in hope.
We forget the barrenness, her branches' bare dead wood;
learn that after death comes resurrection.
Jacaranda claims so, her fugitive colour
uncaught by words,
as she comes to her uplifted blossoming.

# For Alison

Alison Gent 20.09.1920–13.11.2009, feminist and supporter of women's ordination

Jacaranda, you choose your moment
to bloom in glory,
with your feet rooted deep in earth,
your firm trunk,
your arms held wide in blessing.

Your bells ring and flourish
in purple abundance.
With ferny green leaves
you draw white from clouds,
to complete the trinity
of feminist colours,
you feisty woman-tree.

You proliferate softness,
a strong, gentle challenge
to over-arching harshness
we ascribe as blue.

You Advent herald,
you flag of the now,
not yet ecosystem of God.

# Let us look with Christmas eyes

Some avert their eyes,
some stare straight ahead
or look and shrug,
but stay indifferent.
Some have downcast,
despair-ridged faces.
I am selling badges
for the Christmas Bowl
special project this year:
Thai-Burma border refugees.

No one asks me what it's for.
Asians think I'm begging.
My eyes smile in hope,
seek to make contact
with the generous, the kind-hearted.

Further off, a busker seated on the ground,
strums a tinny guitar,
a not-too-tuneful tune, on and on.
I'm glad when he takes a break,
needs his plucking fingers
for a long, long smoke.
'Rolling, rolling, rolling down the river,'
on he goes. Humanity goes rolling on
through Advent to Christmas,
too busy, preoccupied,
not content just to pause and wait
and look with Christmas eyes.

# Thoughts while selling badges for the Christmas Bowl 2013

Cricket fans throng through Topham Link from city hotels
to cross the forty million dollar not-quite-finished
footbridge to the newly refurbished Adelaide Oval.
English or Aussie, they ignore me equally, and I feel guilty
that the guitar playing, singing busker has no chance
of donations. The few who pause to notice choose me
over him. My guilt increases. Then a smartly dressed woman
reassures me. 'He's here every day. Don't worry.'
So I don't, until he leaves guitar and money-hat
on the pavement while he visits the public loo.
But no one cares. He must first have pocketed his few dollars.
Soon he's back, 'Rolling, rolling, rolling like a river,'
he goes, just like last year. Shoppers linger
over books stacked with Christmas trivia
outside the newsagent's. How many get stolen?
I wonder. The Asian owner busies himself inside,
customers coming and going constantly.
My 'clients' give in bursts of generosity,
some pressing notes through the slot in the tin.
Then a lull. I watch a prettily feathered pigeon,
head-bobbing in Egyptian-walk,
pick up crumbs outside Bread Temptation
Vietnamese Patisserie, and Cherry Blossom Sushi Bar,
the bird far more efficient and economic of energy
than the mechanical pavement sweeping machine,
ridden on by a less-than-observant driver.

Does any of this matter, on the day we remember
St Nicholas of Myra, fourth-century bishop
in ancient Asia Minor, modern Turkey,
and his legacy, the legendary Santa Claus?
Yes, for his example of boyhood generosity
when he carved wooden toys for needy children,
his always anonymous kindness to the poor.
On this strange day my fellow badge-seller
later tells me of her mother's death at ninety-nine,
and I must go, willingly, to say the prayers
for her and family. Then comes the news
of another death, Nelson Mandela, Madiba,
at ninety-five, and Desmond Tutu's comment,
'It is not blasphemy to say, He was Christlike.'
I am left pondering on kindness, generosity,
indifference, and who and what is worth remembering.

# At one moment in time and always: the Christmas Eucharist

Finding simple shelter
among humble people
and creatures,
Mary brings her child to birth.
After the hard work,
the bleeding and crying,
she cradles the elemental
human life.
'My body, my blood,'
she laughs and weeps
in relief.
Priests, women and men,
give thanks in belief,
doing this act in remembrance of him,
for the world in which he lived and died
and lived again,
and where he always lives.

# Christmas morning

Cat stays sleeping.
I open the door
on pure, clear air.
Advent's purple petunias
droop, tired.
Red roses topping an arch
catch the sun.
Such special peace today.

### Later

In the silent stillness
of Christmas Day at midnight
I hear the boobook owl
call, 'Look! Look!
On this very day
Emmanuel,
God with us.'

# Sevenhill at Easter

In low, bright light,
I can picture the figure risen,
and the tomb, dark as the crypt
where forty faithful priests and brothers lie,
awaiting resurrection.

Sevenhill at Easter.
Birch gold in the garden,
a claret ash on fire with promise.
The dawn-waking rooster proclaims,
not Peter's betrayal,
but break of day and the stone rolled away
for women and men ready to greet life.

Sevenhill at Easter.
The quest for the empty grave,
and Jesus, in the garden,
and my desire to hold,
and being told,
'You cannot keep me here.
Go to your Galilee.
Make me known to young and old
who seek to know
what this week has been
for you with me:
both frenzy of writing
and serenity of prayer.'

# a tanka for the Triduum*

full Easter moon
floating
round stone
tomb-sealer
transformed
by resurrection light

\* the last three days of Lent: Maundy Thursday to the evening of Holy Saturday

# The reality of God's presence to me

You do not blazon in upon me
like the light of the bedside lamp,
or the red glare of the clock radio's digital figures,
marking the moments.
You are not as clear to me
as the rainwater in my glass,
or the Ginger Water perfume,
my daughter's gift, brought from home.
You do not move the air of my room
or lift the curtain,
but you are here.

You give me words to write,
which themselves are prayer,
and thoughts that fill my mind,
and need rebalancing, transforming.
You do so, God of grace.

You give me the impulse
to read this book, not that.
You speak to me in leaf and flower,
in dappled light,
in age of stone and iron,
the remnants of work and workers gone.

You open my eyes to glimpse a wisp of cloud,
ears to hear the song of bird,
and sharpen all my senses
to be thankful, transcendent one,
intimate one, for the deep I AM
of you. For the thought that's held,
the silence kept,
the stillness. Amen.

# In the Sophia dry-land garden after a week of fires

The air itself is a prayer.
Trees breathe worship,
peppercorns their incense,
a bird their cantor.

My prayer is for remembering
enduring love for the earth
in this place of planted bush,
revering native vegetation,
dedicated to the Kaurna tribes
and to those lost from fire:
people, animals, flora, birds.

Here, bark crackles with footfall,
breeze tenderly moves leaves.
Ants begin their removal
of the fallen blackbird,
all in nature's cycle,
now no firestorm raging.

# Day of the Magdalen

For Madeleine, and Mary of Magdala

In Solemn High Mass on her feast day
our senses are rich with candle glow:
the incense of Arabia,
the liturgy's dignified words,
full bellow of organ,
loud chant of choir.
At the shrine her statue
wears a festal robe.
The guest preacher speaks
of legends conflated
to vision this woman,
apostle to the apostles,
chosen to bring to the men
news from the open tomb,
the Christ's resurrection:
'Mary,' 'Rabbouni.' 'Go. Tell them.'

After shared supper,
as we walk to our cars
in the old city street
incongruously my mobile rings.
'You have a new granddaughter,'
my daughter tells me
in a strained, weary voice.
'Madeleine Emily.' I gasp
at the French for Magdalen,
tell her of the feast day and how
I love the names she has chosen.
'And I didn't even know,' she says,

nonchalantly. The younger generation
seem to miss God's subtle workings.
But grandmothers
are open to all possibilities.

# Wedding music

Oboe and piano join
in the tiny church
on the ridge above cherry orchards.
The bride wears intricate lace,
the gown made by her mother.
Pardalotes nesting in the vestry air vent
respond to the music
with chatter and song.
A glorious celebration in summer's light.

# Tanka: six months after the flood

caught by the camera
and garlanded with willow twigs
a piano floats on its back
the tsunami
playing its tune

# Teacher

I heard a definition of teaching
on the radio: 'facilitating discovery'.
I think of teaching as imparting
what is dear to me,
sharing what I love,
passing on what matters,
is valuable, gives pleasure.

At times, teaching
is presenting something to be known,
instructing in a process,
giving both sides of an argument,
or a view I don't agree with.

Teaching is also an act
when the teacher,
confronted by a classroom
full of the eager
or the indifferent,
must overcome her natural shyness,
fill herself with enthusiasm,
sweep them up
in the desire to learn.

Sometimes, in a rare moment,
teaching is the giving of the soul.
It leaves her drained,
quietly exultant.
Their eyes shine,
their hearts grateful
for sharing discovery.

# To drown or not to drown

A great wave of foam rolls over.
Helpless, I seem to shunt forward,
am threatened by crushing surf.
A false sense of motion deceives me.
Some robotic power to cleanse
creates a frenetic tsunami.

All round me, bundles of kelp
swish, subside, swish, subside.
More foam, a clear wave in pursuit,
spatterings all over, blinding.
A roar, then suddenly silence.

Always the red lights for danger,
like flags on an undertow beach.
After three minutes, the water's
reduced to a trickle only.
GREEN flashes urgent, above me,
'Go! Get going!' it screams.
What relief to drive out of the car wash.

# haiku, tanka, brief glimpses

at C… Youth Training Centre
blue-black Sudanese boys
of the Dinka tribe
find their blond Serbian teacher's name
amusing: it's Dinka

bright lights on a gloomy spring day
red roses glow
among grey wormwood

purple lace parasol
for summer's bride
jacaranda

iceberg rose
flowers on and on
shedding cool in summer air

willow bark
ancient remedy
for pain, fever, inflammation
now refined as aspirin
in small white tablets

purple drifting down –
jacaranda bells
herald Advent, waiting time

# Light upon silk

Standing under the Manchurian pear
I gaze into lace blossom,
silk filaments.
Filigree leaves,
translucent with early sun
clasp water drops
at point of fall.
Where have I seen
such intricacy?

At the display
of Chinese silk embroidery
in the Festival Artspace
I am transfixed
by needlework of finest thread,
each stitch slid perfectly into place.
Silk gives sheen
and subtlety of shade and colour
as mesmerising
as nature flaunting
early spring.

# haiku, tanka, brief glimpses

a dairy farmer, though once gored,
kisses his buffalo
on the nose
and calls him
a good boy

At four in the afternoon
small boy: 'Look, Daddy, the moon.'
'Yes, the moon.'
'And the stars.'
seeing with words and imagination

red yellow flames
in the church
poinsettias for Pentecost

Lek, Thai elephant whisperer,
shows us the eyes empty from abuse
three weeks later
the elephant dies
from human hurt

winter sunset
turns roof lines
to silhouettes
a toy village, a child's drawing

full moon rising
a balloon
trapped in tree branches

# Woman priest to woman dying

In memory of Margaret

no words from you now
so, what will have meaning?
will candle flame?
fragrance of oil?
red roses from my garden?
wood of the cross,
the Christ thin and fixed?
will my words?
the frail disk of bread?
or touch, kiss, and holding?
what will express love, shared?

# The invitation of the spiral

A poem on Sophia as place and holy being

Wend your way inward.
Let your spirit drink
at my fountain centre.
Be refreshed at my gentle heart.
Nestle, and be mothered.
I am tender and strong.

Look up, and bathe in my light.
Let my trees speak to you of change.
What now is winter bare
will re-clothe with new green.
What once was parched
will guild itself with life's learning.

For I am Wisdom,
one with the Creator
from the first moment.
I sense your needs,
and will fulfil them.
Open to me,
for my spiralling way
unfurls with love.

www.ingramcontent.com/pod-product-compliance
Lightning Source LLC
Chambersburg PA
CBHW070048120526
44589CB00034B/1597